Martha Frances

An Altar In Your Heart

Meditations on the Jesus Prayer

Bishop Bob Hibbs

Stillpoint-by-the Sea Books

Stillpoint-by-the-Sea Books
P.O. Box 90016
San Antonio, Texas 78209

Copyright © 1998 by Robert B. Hibbs

ISBN 1-890498-09-2

Edited by Marjorie George
Cover design by Louis Daniel

Printed in the United States of America

For additional copies or catalogs, write:
Stillpoint-by-the-Sea
P.O. Box 90016
San Antonio, Texas 78209

**An audiocassette album of these meditations is also
available. Contact Stillpoint: 1-800-241-2088.**

ACKNOWLEDGEMENTS

When Jenny and Charles Garrett of Stillpoint-by-the Sea first broached the idea of turning the tapes of my retreat addresses on the Jesus Prayer into a small book, I was frankly incredulous. Their confidence and continuing kindly persuasion form the genesis of this work, and I am deeply appreciative.

It is no small feat to turn the idiosyncrasies of my spoken word into written form. I know, because I have tried unsuccessfully on several occasions. Marjorie George, Communications Officer of the Diocese of West Texas, has given more time than I can think of without embarrassment to this task, and her considerable skill has captured the style and cadence of the spoken original. By George, and only by George, this transcription happened. I am deeply grateful.

Nancy Joane Hibbs, my wife and friend of 40 years, is, under God, the foundation of any good thing I may do.

+Bob Hibbs
Epiphanytide, 1998

*Lord
Jesus Christ,
Son of
God,
have
mercy
on me,
a sinner.*

INTRODUCTION

The material in this little book was first presented during a retreat held on the Texas Gulf Coast in 1995. It was a wonderful time of long walks on the beach, listening to waves lap the shore, and watching seagulls retrieve their dinner from the blue waters of the Gulf of Mexico. It was particularly appropriate because the Jesus Prayer itself is a kind of retreat - a little spot of respite from the frantic pace of our late twentieth century.

I invite you to read this material in the posture of a retreat, to amble through it at a leisurely pace, pausing - perhaps for a day or several days - to reflect upon it as you make your way through it.

And I invite you to enter in to a kind of quiet as you allow the material to engage you.

Now, there are two kinds of quiet, and they're not unrelated. The first is what some people call inner quiet. Years ago, I went to seminary in New York City, and nobody's ever thought that New York City was a quiet place. But even in the midst of all that urban din I learned I could be quiet on the inside. I remember once studying for a theology exam in Grand Central Station.

So allow yourself the gift of inner quiet while you read; block out the things of the world and of your life that pull on you for attention. Just let them go for a while; they'll still be there when you get back to them. You'll find that the Jesus Prayer itself is a way to establish inner quiet.

There is also an outer quiet, and that is basically a matter of not talking. I invite you to help yourself to generous intervals of not talking after each period of reading this material. Take your own long walk on the beach, or in the woods, or through the meadow - even if metaphorically - to digest and mull over for a while what you have read.

A second thing to bear in mind as you read is that your thoughts, your reflections, whatever comes to you through the work of the Holy Spirit is every bit as valid and important as anything in the reading. God is the one who is going to do whatever is going to get done. Allow him to speak to you in a very private and personal way through these pages. But don't even work at that too hard; sometimes, you know, prayer is not a matter of saying or doing - it's a matter of being.

The Rt. Rev. Bob Hibbs
San Antonio, Texas

CONTENTS

Chapter One

Origins

It will help us, I think, as we take apart the Jesus Prayer, to first look at it as a whole.

The Jesus Prayer is something that the saints have known for years and years as a venerable method of not just prayer but of being with God, of living in the presence of God. It is one of the primary devotional motifs in Orthodox Christianity - found centuries ago in the Russian church and the Greek church, among others.

The roots of the prayer go right back to the New Testament itself where St. Paul talks about "praying without ceasing" and where we read that no one can say that Jesus is Lord except by the inspiration of the Holy Spirit.

The elements of the Jesus Prayer can be found in the church of the first apostles; but as a developed devotional system, it was during the third and fourth centuries that the prayer began to emerge as a body of doctrine, a body of teaching.

But the Jesus Prayer is not a panacea. It won't cure dandruff, and it won't "magic away" reality. And it's not for everyone. It may occupy a place in your life that is different from the place it occupies in my life. At times it has been a very important part of my spiritual discipleship, and other times it's sort of been in the background. Some people find it becomes almost the centerpiece of their spiritual life; for other people, it might be just one arrow they have in their devotional quiver.

Or the Jesus Prayer may not be for you at all; in that case, pass this book on to someone else and continue your own search for ways of touching God and allowing him to touch you that excite your mind and stroke your heart.

So, this is the Jesus Prayer:
Lord Jesus Christ, son of God,
have mercy on me, a sinner.

That is the basic form. There are variants to that text; some forms don't include "a sinner," so that it is just

**Lord Jesus Christ, son of God,
have mercy on me.**

In its most attenuated form, when it gets all the way down to its roots, it can simply consist of the loving repetition of the holy name of Jesus.

It is a very simple prayer, bringing together in one short sentence, one utterance, two essential moments of Christian devotion: adoration and penitence.

The easiest way to say what's contained in the Jesus Prayer is this: it's Good Friday and it's Easter.

**Lord Jesus Christ, Son of God - Easter;
have mercy on me, a sinner - Good Friday.**

It's always Easter, and it's always Good Friday. You can't have one without the other.

A second thing about the Jesus Prayer is that it's an intensely Christological prayer. That's a 50-cent word theologians use to say that it's intensely focused on Jesus. As we unpack these Christological dimensions, we'll find that the prayer concentrates on both the human person of the incarnate Lord and on his divinity.

When we consider first the incarnation - God taking human form - we have to remember that Christianity is not a gaseous religion: it's not airy, fairy, floaty. Christianity has guts to it, it has armpits, it's got cracked toenails. It's got body parts, and the Jesus Prayer grabs us with the "enfleshedness" of God's love and of our own "enfleshedness." There are many, many patterns of spirituality, but every authentic Christian pattern of spirituality is rooted and grounded in the Incarnation. I would go so far as to say that any pattern of spirituality that is not rooted in the

Incarnation is, to that extent, less than fully Christian.

The richness of the Jesus Prayer is that it also concentrates on the divinity of Jesus. That's why it really is a very orthodox, in every sense of the word, devotion. It's a way of praying our faith in the Incarnation and, at the same time, bowing to the divine.

And yet, the Jesus Prayer is a prayer of utmost simplicity. You really don't need a lot of equipment to "do" it. Sometimes in the morning as I do my walking, I'll use my prayer beads to run through the prayer, but I also use my fingers a lot; I've got ten of them, I can go on forever.

(Even to this day, when a man or a woman becomes a monk or a nun in any one of the Orthodox churches, he or she is given a prayer rope which is a primary tool for developing this unceasing prayer that is such an important part of the religious life in the Orthodox church. The prayer rope is, in fact, much older than the rosary in the Western Church. As an element to move through your fingers as you pray through the Jesus Prayer, the use of a prayer rope goes back to the very beginning of Christian devotion. You might want to try one.)

Or I can sit in a doctor's office and use each person waiting there as a bead. I just drift around the room.

I once read that Cardinal Mindzenty, who was Primate of the Hungarian Church during the horrible time of the Cold War, was arrested and spent years in solitary confinement. When he got out, he was asked, "How did you survive?" And the answer was, "Lord Jesus Christ, son of God, have mercy on me, a sinner."

One of my teachers at the Pontifical Institute, a Dominican priest in Toronto, Canada, was Isadore Eschmann. Father Eschmann was one of those Roman Catholics in Germany during the thirties who refused to go along with

Adolf Hitler. They put Father Eschmann through some horrible exercises. What kept him going? He didn't need a lot of equipment, he didn't need any books: Lord Jesus Christ, son of God, have mercy on me, a sinner.

Almighty and eternal God, so draw our hearts to you, so guide our minds, so fill our imaginations, so control our wills that we may be wholly yours, utterly dedicated to you, and then use us, we pray, as you will, and always to your glory and the welfare of your people. Through our Lord and Savior Jesus Christ, Amen.

Lord Jesus Christ, son of God,
have mercy on me, a sinner. Amen.

Chapter Two

Lord Jesus Christ, Son of God

One of the great journals of Christendom is *Cistercian Studies,* published by the Cistercian fathers, an order in the Roman Catholic church. It was an article which appeared in the journal some time ago that evoked my own interest in the Jesus Prayer, and much of what I know comes from that article. So let's examine the Jesus Prayer a little bit.

The first word in the Jesus Prayer is "Lord." How many times in the course of a week, a day, do we use the word "Lord" in our praying?

Lord Jesus Christ.
Lord Jesus.
Lord, help me.
Lord, Lord, Lord.

It's a remarkable word, Lord. In the Greek it's Kyrie, the vocative form, the address form of the word Kyrios.

In all likelihood, prior to the resurrection nobody ever called Jesus, "Lord." First of all, they wouldn't have called him "Lord" because they didn't use Greek in conversation. They would have spoken Aramaic, maybe occasionally Hebrew.

So they wouldn't have called Jesus "Kyrie." They may have called him "Rabbi" - my teacher.

It was after the resurrection and after the empowering of the church by the Holy Spirit, and most especially after the influx of those non-Jewish people into the church, that this expression - Kyrie, Kyrie, Lord, Lord - would have become part of the common property of the prayer language. Lord is one of the titles of divinity, used even by the pagans in antiquity. They would have talked about Kyrios Apollos - Lord Apollo. Or Kyrios Dionysius, or Kyrios Zeus - Lord Dionysius, Lord Zeus.

But then, in the fullness of time, by his cross and passion, by his glorious resurrection and ascension, and by the coming of the Holy Spirit, Jesus was revealed as the one true Lord.

Thomas, in the upper room, was very close. After that second resurrection appearance in the upper room, it was Thomas who insisted, "Unless I can put my fingers into the wound, unless I can put my hand into the side, I will not, I cannot." And so Jesus, there in that upper room, said, "Thomas, don't be such a schnook, come here, do it." So Thomas did, and then he cried out, in Greek, *"Ho Kyrios mou"* - my Lord - and, *"Ho theos mou"* - and my God. There it is: Lord, Lord.

You see, we need to be very careful we don't get hornswoggled into the cult of sweet Jesus, mild Jesus, wimpy Jesus. We need to not do that, simply because it's not what the New Testament says about him. It's not what the primitive church knew about him. They knew him as king, as royalty, as divinity, as Lord.

His name, as a child, was probably Jehoshua - Joshua. We've Anglicanized it to Jesus.

Jehoshua means "Yahweh is my salvation, Yahweh is my savior."

One reason why Jewish males wear yarmulkes is that any form of the divine name "Yahweh" is so sacred, so holy, that you would not presume to have it uttered without the reverence of a covered head.

I grew up in an Anglican family of strict observance in Philadelphia, and as a child I remember that whenever you said the name of Jesus, you'd bow your head. It's so holy, you'd just bow your head. The ladies used to curtsy whenever they'd hear the name of Jesus. That's the old, strict observance.

Yahweh is my salvation; Yahweh is my savior. That's really what the name Jesus means: savior. It's a name which describes who he is.

Our Medieval sisters and brothers in the faith had a wonderful prayer. It was: Jesus esto mihi Jesus - Jesus be to me a Jesus. Jesus be to me a savior. Savior be to me a savior. Savior be to me a Jesus. It all just sort of flows together. Lord, Jesus. You see it growing?

The second part of the title is Christ - Jesus, the Christ. Christ is the Greek direct translation of the Hebrew word "Messiah." When we say Jesus Christ, we're really saying Jesus, the Messiah. *Jesus Christos*, or as it regularly appears in the New Testament: *Jesus ho Christos*, Jesus, the Christ, Jesus the Messiah. It's a title. If Lord is the title of divinity, Christos is the title of his anointedness.

Do you remember how kings were chosen in ancient history? Samuel was an example of it. There was a terrible conflict in the ancient community of our Jewish ancestors - would they have a king or would they not? Some people absolutely demanded that God give them a king, and other people thought they dare not have a king because the only King to have was Yahweh. Finally, the word of the Lord came to Samuel and he took a vial of oil and poured it out over the head of Saul. It was in that anointing that the Holy Spirit came, the *Ruach Elohim*, the Spirit of God which came upon Saul and he became King of Israel. It was the anointing with the oil that was the occasion, and the word used for what happened to Saul was he became *mashiach*, he became a messiah. He became a christ. And ever after all of the kings - Saul, Solomon, and even Solomon's no-good son, Rehoboam - were all anointed, they were all *mashiach*.

Even after the split, when one of the two kingdoms went to the north and one to the south, and the whole story became a pitiful, sad story of a decline in faith and a decline in obedience and of exile and captivity, even those insignificant little kings were *mashiach* - they were anointed.

Then in the fullness of time, there came One who did not speak the words about God, but who was himself the Word made flesh. At his baptism in the river Jordan, the Spirit came upon him. It was the outpouring of the Spirit of the living God, that Spirit which brooded in the beginning of all time. And he was *mashiach* and King, anointed. Lord Jesus Christ, anointed Son of God. The Council of Chalceden, in 451 A. D., put it this way:

"Therefore following the holy fathers we all with one accord teach men to acknowledge one and the same Son, our Lord Jesus Christ, at once complete in Godhead and complete in manhood, truly God, truly man, consistent also of a reasonable soul and body, of one substance with the Father as regards his Godhead, and at the same time, of one substance with us, as regards his manhood, like us in all respects apart from sin, as regards his Godhead, begotten of the Father before the ages, but yet as regards his manhood, begotten for us men and for our salvation of Mary the Virgin, the God bearer, one and the same Christ, Son, Lord, only begotten, recognized in two natures without confusion, without change, without division, without separation, the distinction of natures being in no way annulled by the union, but rather the characteristics of each nature being preserved and coming together to form one person and subsistence, not as parted or separated into two persons but one and the same son, and only begotten God, the Word, Lord Jesus Christ. Even as the prophets from earliest times spoke of him, and our Lord Jesus Christ himself taught us and the creed of the fathers was handed down to us."

This is God, who from the beginning before creation, in

the tremendous loving dynamism and power of what that word "God" means, was throbbing with love and energy. What proceeds from him is the Eternal Word of God, the divine self knowledge, that thing, that being, which shares all of God's creative power and energy and beauty and majesty and dominion. The Word of God. What God knows about God. That's the son, S-O-N. That's the Son of God in his uncreated, consubstantial, coeternal splendor. All of those big, heavy words.

And then, in the fullness of time, for love of us - and love of all of us in every time and every place getting very, very small and helpless, and in a time and in a place and in a manger becoming one with us. Son of God - very, very, very big and very, very, very small.

Lord Jesus Christ, Son of God.

That's the ecstasy of the Jesus Prayer.

It's the Easter part, it's the Alleluia part. And what a universe of theology, what a universe of experience is compressed into that. You see, it's really a kind of embryonic creed. It has to do with creation; it has to do with incarnation; it has to do with resurrection. All that the church has been doing, and really all that the church will ever do, is just kind of meditate and reflect, and meditate and reflect, and meditate and reflect the Lord Jesus Christ as Son of God.

Direct us, O Lord, in all our doings with your most gracious favor, and further us with your continual help; that in all our works begun, continued, and ended in you, we may glorify your holy Name, and finally, by your mercy, obtain everlasting life; through Jesus Christ our Lord. Amen. (From the Book of Common Prayer, 1979.)

**Lord Jesus Christ, Son of God,
Have mercy on me, a sinner.**

Chapter Three
Have Mercy On Me, a Sinner

I get offended by some of the pop theology which is all over the place, the theology of paperback books that talks about God, "my cosmic buddy."

Sure, there's a sense in which I do need God as my companion. But God is not just the manager of the celestial country club. And when ultimately I see God, I'm not going to walk up and say, "Good morning, God, it's a pleasure to meet you, I am profoundly honored."

No. I like the ancient words of the Eucharist better: "Therefore with angels and archangels and with all the company of heaven . . ." Whenever we say that, you can see the whole church bowing down in profound adoration as it says, "Holy, Holy, Holy, Lord God."

The more I know who God is, and I never, never have perfect knowledge, and then the more I know who I am, the more I know what I want from God: mercy, patience, love.

I have a friend who is an Episcopal priest and about an umpteenth generation Texan, who had an aunt named Lonnie. Apparently, she was the terror of the family - one of these really poisonous, passive-aggressive people who just broke other people wherever she went. You know the kind: "If you love me, you will..." All of the family belonged to the Umbadumblian Church, except for this weird guy who turned out to be a priest in a church that sounded like Pepsi-Cola spelled sideways. Anyway, Aunt Lonnie died, and so it seemed only appropriate to have the priest say something. So there they all were at this neat little cemetery by the riverside, and they sang *Amazing Grace* and all that good stuff. Then my friend got up and he stood by the hole where Aunt Lonnie's body was and he said, "If God is a God of justice only, Aunt Lonnie is in Hell right now."

And that's the truth. But it's not just the truth for Aunt

Lonnie, it's the truth for all of us. If God is a God of justice only, there is no good news, there's nothing. What we need is mercy. We absolutely need it; without it, we cannot stand. Without it, we cannot live.

The beautiful thing is that when we ask God for mercy, we are not pleading with God to give us something he is reluctant to give. It is God's joy and God's delight, the essence of who he is, to give us what we plead for. And so the cry of the Jesus prayer is not a cry for "Oh, I hope he will do it," but "Oh, he does it, over and over and over again." It is the mercy of God, the grace of God, and his lovely transubstantiating power that takes the bread and wine of my life, and of all of our lives, and blesses it and breaks it and recreates it to make it more than it could ever, ever, ever be. All of that is grace and all of that is mercy. And it's the stream we swim in. "Have mercy" is not just a heart-rending petition; it's an outburst of our experience. We cry to the God of mercy for mercy. It's our breath, it's our life, it's our water, it's our air. Have mercy on me. Who is me?

Some of us have a horrible time with "me." We fly on a kind of a trapeze between two "me's." One is god-like, a me that is the product of illusion and delusion, an arrogant me, a me who is powerful, a me who is self-sufficient, a me who is grandiose, a me who is self-will run riot, a me who will trample over people I love and devour them and consume them. A me who wants what I want when I want it, a me who is pathological and pathogenic. A me who is sick as hell.

If that me is the grandiose phony, the other me is the grandiose negative phony.

"I'm nothing, I'm a worm, oh God, oh God," this one goes. And we sway and we stagger back and forth between the two.

In the Jesus Prayer we talk about me, the real me, the creature me, the one who is not absolute, in any way. The one who is limited, the one who is real, the one who can love, but who needs help to love; the one who can know, but who needs help to know; the one who can will and does will in a limited, created way; but the one who needs help to will the good and avoid the evil. But above all, the me who is at every moment loved by God, who is the apple of God's eye. Who, when I walk through the valley of the shadow of death, will be with me and in me and for me.

Be merciful, have mercy upon the real me. Because I am not a worm, but a sinner. I am broken; I'm busted.

There's a lot of American religion that is kind of turning into a sort of religious cheerleading. And it works up to a point. I get inspired, I get the warm fuzzies of religious enthusiasm. I go to retreats and come away shouting, "Excelsior!"

The difficulty is if I just trust me, there is no god I will not blaspheme, no truth I will not dishonor, and no good I will not betray. And I know that, and I cannot pull myself up by my own bootstraps. I'm not the little engine that thought it could. I need help.

Jesus said to his disciples, and that includes us, "Without me, you can do nothing." I need Jesus, I need God's grace, I need the Father and the Son and the Holy Spirit - not as a pious option, not as a second mile of religious devotion. I need help to be the real me. That's what it means to be a sinner. I just need help. And God says, " I know you do. And good you know it. You need it and I'll do it."

Wonderful prayer, theologically rich, psychologically profound: Lord Jesus Christ, Son of God, be merciful to me, a sinner.

Lord, make us instruments of your peace. Where there is hatred, let us sow love. Where there is injury, pardon. Where there is discord, union. Where there is doubt, faith. Where there is despair, hope. Where there is darkness, light. Where there is sadness, joy. Grant that we may not so much seek to be consoled as to console; to be understood as to understand; to be loved as to love. For it is in giving that we receive; it is in pardoning that we are pardoned; and it is in dying that we are born to eternal life.

Lord Jesus Christ, Son of God,
have mercy on me, a sinner.

CHAPTER FOUR

Making it Yours:
Working with the Jesus Prayer

The first thing you have to do if you're going to use the Jesus Prayer is at some point say, " I will try it." There has to be that assent of the will. You know what it is, you're finding out a little bit about it and so it's not just an ineffable mystery, it's a way to pray, and you have to say, "I will try it."

There's another equally good response and that is, "I will not try it."

Either way is good. The Jesus Prayer is not the only way to salvation. It's not the only way to sanctity. It's a possibility; it's a good possibility, but it may not feel right for you.

I know for myself, the first time I heard about it I was fascinated by it, but it was kind of a little bit spooky, a little too far out, and I think I really wasn't ready. So I had to say, "Thanks, but no thanks." And that may be the case for you. What we need to avoid, all of us need to avoid, is spiritual dilettantism: the mentality of Jesus Prayer one week and spiritual growth through drinking carrot juice the next. I don't know any serious spiritual writer or spiritual teacher who recommends that.

One of my good friends is St. Benedict, whose Rule is the basis of a whole household of spirituality. In his Rule, Benedict talks about detestable monks, which is pretty strong. They even have a kind of ugly name, they are the *gyrovagues*. Like a gyroscope that is running down, they stumble and stagger around, going from one monastery and spiritual director to the next. In our own day, there's a lot of that. There are people, for instance, who become addicted to retreating - the only time they ever come alive is when they go on a retreat and get turned on by whatever or whoever is the star of that particular show for that particular weekend.

That's spiritually unhealthy. It's a "feel good-ism." It's searching for the tingle, and it's selfish. It becomes a kind of fascination with religious feelings. Ultimately, all spirituality is tested not by whether it feels good, but to what extent it impels us into apostolic action, to what extent it forces us to come to grips with the imperative to be Christ in the environment in which we find ourselves.

We're always in danger, especially if we think we are spiritually superior, of becoming cesspools of grace. It just flows in, and it flows in, and it flows in, and it never flows out. We're always sort of sucking it up, but we never, never get to being Christ in the environment.

The Al Anon people have a phrase - "Try 90 meetings in 90 days, and if that doesn't work, we'll refund your misery." I like that. If you really want to find out something about the Jesus Prayer, take off a nice chunk of time, like 90 days, and say, "For the next three months, I'm going to really see if this is for me." Try it, and grow with it. Check in with your spiritual director or with your parish priest and if he or she is in favor, give it the old college try.

I once said to a group of people that I'm not really interested in books that were written after the invention of printing. What I meant was there is a problem related to our easy access to unlimited numbers of religious books. The Rev. Dr. Von Schlugenbugen makes a pronouncement and everybody goes off on a tangent, and you read and you read. We get into the mode of any spiritual thrill that you can thrill I can thrill better.

Be careful of that. It can result in a kind of superficiality. Every one of us sooner or later is going to have to go through the real thing. For sure. There's death, and there's dying, and there's sin, and there's tough stuff out there. And that's when some of that light stuff that floats on the surface will betray you. It's like a life jacket that's lost its buoyancy. Real spirituality is very valuable. As you begin to work with the Jesus Prayer, be certain you're approaching it with some solid intention: "I will try it," or, equally good, "It's interesting, but it's not for me." And that's fine.

The Jesus Prayer in the beginning really is an oral prayer. You have to say the words aloud. I encourage you to find some place where you can do that with some degree of abandon. Say it with all of your muscles, with your fingernails, and your toenails, and your belly button. To just reduce the prayer to a kind of a thinky, thoughty kind of thing neglects the lovely thing that God has created. So, get out there and stride along. And when nobody's looking - because, after all, we are all kind of uptight - just do it. You'll be fine.

Now a second element in the beginning is deliberate acts of the will that fix the attention on the prayer. You could observe, "Well, it's now 4:25, and for the next five minutes, I'm going to do it." Just be kind of tough. If we wait around until we're inspired to pray, the chances are real good that we're going to be cheapskate pray-ers. I don't know about you, but I don't get up in the morning and throw open the window and shout, "Alleluia." On Sunday mornings I don't think, "Oh, blessed be thou, Lord God, king of the universe, now I get to go to church." No, no, no. It doesn't work like that. It's morning and I'm a responsible human being, I've been ordained to do certain things, and it's got nothing to do with how I feel about it. It is my bounden duty as a Christian to do x and y and z, my bounden duty as a priest to do x and y and z. So womanfully or manfully I pledge to do five minutes of the Jesus Prayer. In the tradition of the Jesus Prayer, quantity is also important in the beginning.

Are you old enough to have learned to drive in a conventional shift car with a clutch? Aren't you glad you learned to do that? Once you got the hang of it, it was really neat. But do you remember learning to do it? Oh boy, if there ever was an exercise in patting your head and rubbing your tummy at the same time. You had to think your way - now I will depress the clutch, and now pull it down here, then let out the clutch and give it the gas and it goes, and put in the clutch. . . . And it was awful, just awful. You had to do it many, many times until it became second nature. Eventually you got so good you could downshift to slow the car down. And then you could stop it and hold it on a steep hill. Remember all that? The only way you developed that facility is because you'd done it enough times. Even now, sometimes, I really like it when the rental car is a stick-shift.

That's the way it is with the Jesus Prayer. You practice, you do it without thinking.

Or use your breathing: on the inhale say, "Lord Jesus Christ, son of God," and on the exhale, "Have mercy on me, a sinner."

In all of it, relax. Spirituality, good spirituality, healthy spirituality usually has a little element of playfulness. If you find yourself getting terribly white knuckled, ease up. If you find yourself hyperventilating quit it. Play a little. Enjoy.

When you first begin to use the Jesus Prayer, you're going to be distracted. You just cannot help but be distracted. Get ready for it. You'll start to pray then find yourself thinking about everything. Or you'll begin to worry about what's going to happen next week, and what's going to happen next month. Always that static goes on. Always, always.

I want to make a suggestion about distraction in prayer in general, and distraction in prayer with the Jesus Prayer.

Don't be impatient with yourself. If you find yourself saying, "Oh, I did it again," stop all that. Of course you did it again. It doesn't mean you're wicked and it doesn't mean you're bad, it just means that you're human. Gently, gently, when you find yourself distracted in prayer, gently turn away from the distraction. Gently. One of the great spiritual writers says - and this is kind of ponderous, but it's kind of lovely - that when you find yourself distracted from your prayer, say, "I have turned aside from my prayer. I will return to my prayer."

Now my final statement is - and this is a quote from one of those old, bearded Russian fathers - "The attentive repetition of the prayer often proves a hard and exhausting task, calling for humble persistence." I don't know anybody who's into the Jesus Prayer who hasn't gone through humble persistence. Stick to it, humbly, persistently, gently, not arrogantly.

So, it's oral prayer, and it requires deliberate acts of the will: "I'm going to do it, I'm going to do it for the next five minutes, for the next ten minutes. And I'm going to do it over and over and over again." And humble persistence.

Then the next step is that in time the prayer becomes inward. It's going to take you a while to get to step two, but there are some indicators that let you know when this is happening. The oral part, the moving of the lips and the tongue, becomes less important. You can still do it, and you'll want to do it, but the prayer is going even when you're not doing that. It doesn't require the mechanics of your lips.

The concentration of the attention becomes easier. Once my wife said to me, "Bob, quit praying the Jesus Prayer while you're driving, because you're starting to wander off the road." And she was right.

Thirdly, and this is very significant, the prayer gradually acquires a rhythm of its own. Not always the same rhythm, but it comes. In the morning when I'm walking, without my knowing it I'll begin to realize that the prayer is just bouncing along with the cadence of my body's movement. It develops this rhythm. It may begin to relate to the way I'm breathing, or it may pick up the rhythm of my heartbeat.

Eventually, the prayer enters the heart. The rhythm is identified more and more closely with the movement of the heart until it becomes unceasing. It just goes on and on and on and it never stops. It has entered the heart, and as long as the heart is beating, the heart is praying the Jesus Prayer. And what was originally something that required painful and strenuous effort is now an inexhaustible source of peace and joy.

But you can't worry about "attaining" the third stage. It's God's gift, it will come. Be persistent in stage one and stage two and sooner or later in time or eternity, it will be all right. Just don't worry about it. The overwhelming majority of people who practice the Jesus Prayer are in the first and second stage . There's an old Baptist hymn that says, "Take time to be holy." Holiness requires taking time. There is no instant holiness. It takes time. Lots of prayer, lots of meditations, lots of confessions, lots of communions - it takes time. It's part of our world's problem with sanctity - we live in a world where you just add water and you've got soup, you've got coffee. There's no mystical, magical hooha powder you can put into a cup and add water and stir and you drink it and it will make you holy. It won't work. So, don't worry about the third stage - it's God's gift. Take time. A lifetime.

Some observations: Avoid worrying about concepts and images. When I was in seminary, we had a visiting English bishop come and give us a course in meditating. He was using a gospel story which occurred in a boat, and he said, "Picture Jesus in a boat." Well, most of my life I have had lousy vision, so visual imaging is not my long suit, and I could no more picture Jesus in a boat than I could fly by flapping my ears.

After class I went to the bishop and I said, "Bishop, I'm a goner, because I cannot picture Jesus in a boat." And he laughed at me because I was such an earnest little guy. Then he said, "Well, what can you do? Does the sense of the presence of God mean anything to you." And I said, "Well, yes, sure. One night when I was very young, while Mama and I were doing the 'Now I lay me down to sleep,' and the 'God blesses,' I had this feeling that there was someone else in the room with us. So after Mama had left the room, I climbed out of bed and got down on my knees and did my prayers again to see if the someone was still there, and he was. And that was the beginning of something."

"Well," said the bishop, "never mind all this picture stuff. Just be in the presence."

The Jesus Prayer is about contemplation, about being in the presence of God.

My wife and I dated for a long time before getting married. I remember that when we first began to date, we had so much to talk about. Talk, talk, talk, talk. And we had so much in common. We were very busy together. But eventually we were content to just be with each other. We had a favorite pizzeria, and we'd go there and just hold hands across the pizza.

A lot of prayer is busyness. You have these lists, you have rules of life, you say Morning Prayer and Evening Prayer and Wednesday nights and all of that.

The Jesus Prayer is not so much being busy as it is being in a mutual relationship of loving regard between you and Jesus. Just hold hands across the pizza.

But the Jesus Prayer also presupposes some things. It presupposes living in grace as a vital, living member of the body of Christ. It presupposes regular communion, regular confessions, other prayers. It presupposes singing in the choir, working on the altar guild, being regular at church, all of that stuff. The Jesus Prayer is not the prayer of a spiritual lone ranger; it's the prayer of somebody who is deeply imbedded in the life of grace, in the risen life of Christ.

Assist us mercifully, O Lord, in these our supplications and prayers, and dispose the way of your servants toward the attainment of everlasting salvation; that, among all the changes and chances of this mortal life, they may ever be defended by your gracious and ready help; through Jesus Christ our Lord. Amen. (From the Book of Common Prayer, 1979.)

Lord Jesus Christ, Son of God, have mercy on me, a sinner.

CHAPTER FIVE
Focusing the Jesus Prayer

One of the basic concepts about the Jesus Prayer that is difficult - not because it's really difficult, but because it's new and unusual - is the idea of the prayer in the heart. The Eastern Orthodox have been at it for 2000 years now, but for Westerners it's harder to comprehend, and it begins with asking, "Where is Jesus?" Right away you will say, "everywhere," or, "he's in heaven." But both of those answers have residual problems: If you say "everywhere," that is too diffuse. We're not everywhere, we're right here. How do we get him here? I have the same problem with Jesus being located in heaven.

I think we have to recognize that one of the things that makes Christianity different from the other religions is its "physicalness," its "fleshiness," its "stuffness." It comes to us out of the Jewish womb from which we were born. As soon as we say with St. John, "In the beginning was the Word, and the Word was God, and all things were made by him and without him was not anything made that was made . . and the Word became flesh and dwelt among us," as soon as we've said that, we've said something that's uniquely Christian. And we've said something that means that all of our thinking about spirituality has to be incarnational spirituality, has to be fleshly spirituality, has to be sacramental spirituality, and we've got to be able to say something about where Jesus is in terms of other than in heaven.

Jesus is in all created things, he is in other people, other human beings, however defaced by sin. He's in us; he's in me.

Jesus is the creative word of God by whom all things were made. Do you remember the Genesis story? The word of God that comes roaring forth and says, "Let there be . . . " and there is. There is not a thing in the room where you sit right now - nothing - that is not sustained in being by the word of God. The chair that's supporting your weight is a creature. It's a lovely creature. It's being sustained in being right this moment. Physics teaches us that there's tremendous energy and power in the chair that's holding you up. There is a tremendous dynamism. It's not just a static lump of stuff. My goodness, there's enough stuff in your chair to blow up six worlds. It's throbbing with being. And the reason it's throbbing with being is that the Creative Word is sustaining it in being. Now do you know what's going to happen to you if God stops being present in the chair you're sitting on? You're going to fall on your fanny.

Now, for a moment, focus your attention - your prayer, if you will, the presence of the Word of God, the Word made flesh in Jesus - on some created thing. Pick anything - your shoelace, your cross, your pencil, your chair. Just grab hold of that thing with your senses. Embrace some created thing with as many of the senses as you conveniently can do. Be aware of it. The Word of God made flesh in Jesus of Nazareth is present in that thing, sustaining it in being.

See, the heavens do declare the glory of God, and the firmament does show forth his handiwork. Tonight you can go out and embrace a star, worship and adore the word of God present in the spacious firmament on high. Sure. But you don't have to be nearly as grandiose as that. You can reach into your pocket and hold a piece of chewing gum. It, no less than the spacious firmament on high, declares the presence of the One who sustains it in being.

We live in a radically sacramental universe. I often think the presence of God is like when you cover your eyes with your hands, and it's not that your hands aren't there, it's just that they're too close. God has impregnated himself in his creation. It's the divine closeness that's the problem, not the divine absence . We have to back off from it in